YOUR KNOWLEDGE HAS VALUE

- We will publish your bachelor's and master's thesis, essays and papers

- Your own eBook and book - sold worldwide in all relevant shops

- Earn money with each sale

Upload your text at www.GRIN.com and publish for free

Bernadette Maria Kaufmann

Technology Enhanced Learning as a tool for eInclusion and Media

GRIN Publishing

Bibliographic information published by the German National Library:

The German National Library lists this publication in the National Bibliography; detailed bibliographic data are available on the Internet at http://dnb.dnb.de .

Imprint:

Copyright © 2010 GRIN Verlag, Open Publishing GmbH
Print and binding: Books on Demand GmbH, Norderstedt Germany
ISBN: 978-3-656-13167-0

This book at GRIN:

http://www.grin.com/en/e-book/175943/technology-enhanced-learning-as-a-tool-for-einclusion-and-media

GRIN - Your knowledge has value

Since its foundation in 1998, GRIN has specialized in publishing academic texts by students, college teachers and other academics as e-book and printed book. The website www.grin.com is an ideal platform for presenting term papers, final papers, scientific essays, dissertations and specialist books.

Visit us on the internet:

http://www.grin.com/

http://www.facebook.com/grincom

http://www.twitter.com/grin_com

Keywords: community, digital knowledge, learning, Constructivism, media and society

Bernadette Maria Kaufmann

Technology Enhanced Learning as a tool for eInclusion and Media

Introduction

In this contribution I'd like to present to you a short overview of eInclusion from two perspectives. I start with the example of a student's learning situation in a private school, then in contrast going on with illuminating most students' situation in public schools.
Then I consider a constructivist view of learning as an adequate pedagogic strategy for "new schools" that aim at helping students develop good competence in ICT and media perception.

There are two perspectives in the center of this text:
1) eInclusion focusing students:
Students from ALL social backgrounds should have the opportunity of including ICTS into their lifes , develop skills in this field and also in the field of media competencies.
Next to the view onto the development of skills in using ICT and the importance of helping students develop media-competencies, I'd like to consider a constructivist view of learning (and teaching).
2.) in my opinion it's necessary to include poverty as a topic also for students.

The inclusion of poverty in media contexts is of high importance to me and in the center of a scientific debate I am working out at the moment.
Social (e)Inclusion in my opinion also contains that we do not only try to include the poor into social partake, but also make poverty visible which is the first step to make a change for the better.

CYBERHOMEWORK - a student's learning situation in a private school

Austria in 2009:

„I enjoy doing cyber-homework a lot", says Max, 10 years. "It's fun!"
Max attends a private school. Cyber-homework in subjects like English is
standard.
Students of his school have the opportunity of using ICT - computers are
integrated in various subjects: for instance, they often can try CD-ROMS
and use computers in geography, and of course homework for, let's say,
biology can be done on computer, using ICT for finding out about different
tasks.
They are doing different kind of small "projects" that way.
Investigating about the number of a certain kind of insects in combination
with book and Wikipedia can be lots of fun!
Studying gets exciting this way.

Max has been working a lot with computers and different media for several
years. He started in pre-school at the age of 3 years, starting with about 15
to a maximum of 20 minutes per session.
This worked out very well.
He now is an expert who can easily use ICT and enjoys finding out more
about the world he is part of.
Max is privileged:
He attends a private school that offers a wide range of possibilities and that
has an excellent image.
Many lessons take place in small groups of students, in many subjects
(languages and natural sciences) Max and his classmates are divided into
small groups, each group of students having a teacher of their own.

But what about children, that attend a public school?
Education in public schools does in most cases look different than in the
example above.
Children that do not attend a private school and that don't derive from a
family that are good educated and use ICT in their careers as well as in
their private life are disadvantaged this way, because they don't learn a
reasonable way of dealing with ICT, of recognizing risks and opportunities
in this context.
That way they are neither at home nor at school confronted with a
reasonable and "success-oriented" use of ICT.

"Children are our future" is a motto often heard.
Private schools are in a better economical position, but what about the
public ones?

Is it alright, that some children are privileged, and those deriving from poor families, or families that are not that wealthy, in some way "loose"?
It is important to keep in mind, that not every parent notices how important a really good education is for every child, and that not every one is wealthy enough to send their child to a language school for instance to take English classes there, because the local elementary school does NOT teach English, even though it is obliged to do so!

In the recent years Austrian public schools had less money than needed, as it seems.
Even though there are initiatives in Austria like EDUmoodle that try to integrate technological enhanced learning into education and young people's lives, and there are also concerned teachers that are trying to improve learning conditions for "their" students on their own.
This lack of enough money for the inclusion of pupils from all social backgrounds into achieving knowledge and experience concerning the use of ICT affects our future society. If it's not able to make a change, children from certain social backgrounds will be left behind and therefore are very likely to suffer from different disadvantages concerning their personal developments in fields of further education, social statuses and careers.
In the end it affects all of us: it affects economy and therefore European Society.

Also these children are members of our knowledge-society.
They have the right to take part and as Hasebrink et al. point out:
"As the rise in new technologies leads towards network or knowledge societies, schools have an important role in strengthening children's competencies in dealing with the opportunities and risks associated with ICT" (Livingston 2009, 217 ff.).

2009 ICT has already moved into Austrian schools, but further improvements are necessary.
Schools have the responsibility of helping students develop their skills in using ICT and online learning, and supporting the development of students' media-competence is also most important.

ICT AND SCHOOLS

According to the report on data availability and research gaps in Europe within the project "EU Kids Online" Paus-Hasebrink says there are two

statements that can be made about "ICT and Schools" (Livingston 2009, 220):
More research is needed on the role of teachers (relating to various categories), and second, in her opinion many European countries lack an evidence base regarding online learning.
For an overview of available studies concerning ICT and schools Paus-Hasebrink and her team filtered relevant studies within the EU Kids Online data repository (see www.lse.ac.uk/collections/EUKidsOnline/).

She made a pan-European comparison about European kids' use of internet in and for school:
"On average, European children use the internet more in the home (67%) than in school (57%); moreover, the more they use it at home, the more they also use it at school" (Livingston 2009, 221 ff.).

Young people use internet mainly for school, but it's also of growing importance in their private lives - they use it "as an educational resource, for entertainment, games and fun, searching for information, social networking and sharing experiences with others" (Hasebrink et al, 2009).

She found there are differences in kids' internet access in school and grouped countries into four categories:
Those with the least in-school internet access are Lithuania, Greece, Romania, Bulgaria, Italy and Spain (proportion accessing internet varies between 25% and 37%).
The proportion accessing the internet in school are between 44% and 56% in Estonia, Cyprus, Latvia, Belgium, Slovenia, Ireland, Germany, Portugal, France and Malta.
In Poland, Austria, Finland, Slovak Republic, Sweden, Czech Republik, the Netherlands and Hungary this proportion lies between 61% and 75%.
With 81% and 89% Denmark and the UK are the highest.

"Concerning the equipment of European schools... in most of the European countries there are no central regulations fixing a maximum number of pupils per computer, and decisions concerning investments in IT equipment are taken at a local level"(Ibid.)

She suggests that school should provide "a learning environment where pupils deal with topics that fit in their ,life worlds' , wherein media play a relevant role and an authentic information and communication space is provided (Paus-Hasebrink et al, 2007, 89). Fascinating students with the reality of media techniques through using wikis in schools, for example, can strengthen their motivation of learning".

She also points out that different changes are necessary (adequate pedagogic strategies , a learner-centred approach, etc.).

CONSTRUCTIVISM
A constructivist view of learning

One adequate pedagogic strategy for "new schools" is a constructivist view of learning.
"Constructivism... is a theory about learning" (Reiter et al 2001, 53), it is "a philosophy and a cognitive, developmental psychology that explains learning as a case of interpreting and inferring about the world. Meaning is understood to be the result of human setting up relationships, reflecting on their actions, and modelling and constructing explanations" as well as "...learning needs to be understood as the individual development of strategies, ,big ideas' and models, but within a cultural and social community"(Ibid.).

As Catherine Twomey Fosnot explains, there's been a major reform taking place that stems from a constructivist view of learning in classroom-reform over the last ten years (note: this comment was made 2001!).
The glimpse into a classroom she offers shows that learning AND teaching will look very different if teaching supports cognitive construction (Reiter at al 2001, 54 ff.).
This "glimpse into a classroom" shows how interesting maths can become for students under this constructivist view of learning:
The classroom becomes a workshop, they are constructing meaning, also using technology as a tool.

This means an important shift from conventional teaching (Twomey Fosnot speaks here of behaviourism) to new roles of teachers and their students.

The teacher's role can be described as supportive of growth by questioning and providing examples, asking students to generalize and convince each other.
These examples can very well relate to or derive from the children's world for achieving better understanding.
The classroom, as she writes, becomes in some way a "mini-society - a community of learners engaged in mathematical activity, discourse, and reflection... Learners share perceptions with each other and with the teacher, and their ideas become modified or reinforced as common meanings develop. This enables learners to become clearer and more

confident of what they know and understand. Constructivism describes learning as ‚cognitive re-organization' " (Reiter at al 2001, 57).

This idea of teaching in a sort of "workshop-situation" opens new perspectives for young people.
It's not only a most suitable way of learning and teaching e.g. maths - it might also be an excellent way of helping children and teenagers from ALL backgrounds develop more competence in using ICT and develop a good perception of different media.

TEL and Media:
POVERTY AS A MEDIA EXPERIENCE

As mentioned before, media play a prominent role in society.
They are a tool we use for the constitution of the world we live in, media help us receive and organize information about our world and:
They are opinion makers!

Their importance must not be underestimated.
Media decide how we see things in our world - because we use them for our construction of meaning.
And therefore it is important to keep this in mind, to know "their game" and not be in the worst case really "deceived" by news that media make.

Technology Enhanced Learning should also include leading pupils to a reasonable way of using media. In my opinion we cannot exclude this topic from other learning content that is considered as important or even very important.
When we agree that web 2.0 / social web is the future as well as technology enhanced learning in general, we have to find a way to include the training of skills in media reception and social learning to some instant as well.

As a communication scientist I suggest, also teachers should make their students aware what role media have come to play in our lives, and that a lot of content shown on the media of every kind - no matter, if we are talking about television, papers or also web 2.0, the so called "social web" and its specific forms of "new media" - is in some way often "some kind of creation", a mise-en-scène, it is what we call in German "Inszenierung".
To develop media-competencies as early as possible is really important - in my opinion this also contains the ability of calling into question…

Reality is not media-reality, the presentation of "real things" can be ambivalent.
Children should also be made aware of this - they are in the position of "digital natives", they are the youngest members in our knowledge society. And, most of all, children should be encouraged to develop the ability of critical thinking. They must become able to challenge something, to call something into question.

How can we train them?
As presented above, this is most important to become part of the curriculum in schools.
That's certainly a job left to parents/ family, but as well teachers.
We always have to keep in mind that not all members of our knowledge society have the same resources and possibilities concerning digital tools, "social web" and so on. Some even don't have a computer, not to begin speaking of the access to internet.

Schools should therefore be provided with technology to make sure that in future more people gain access to internet, technology enhanced learning and the "social web".

LEARNING MANGEMENT SYSTEM:
CAN MEDIA BE A PART OF IT?

Depending on the aims, on the goals that shall be reached in education, starting at the level of elementary-school, we could turn this question around:
Why can't media be part of Learning Management Systems?
We can include media that show "real life" as well as to some extend scientists' publications, depending on the age and knowledge-background of kids of course, to make students find out about different topics like historical events or the European Union, but also about "real life" and social topics.
Some schools already do this (see my example in the beginning!).

Gaining the ability of "investigating the web" is of high importance.
Web-based Learning Management Systems could help combining multiple sources for students' online-learning:

> *"Unter einer webbasierten Lernplattform ist*
> *eine serverseitige installierte Software zu verstehen,*
> *die beliebige Lerninhalte über das Internet vermitteln hilft*
> *und die Organisation der dabei notwendigen Lernprozesse unterstützt."*

(Baumgartner et al, 2002)

If using Wikipedia can be considered as a great tool also in education, why can't we let children work on a topic also using media that show information on a certain social topic, reading about it in small work-groups maybe, discussing the content and then finding to questions that occur important to them?

In my opinion this could happen in schools, in various subjects like history, geography, also languages and ethics.
For instance, in English it's already "standard" having pupils do their Cyber-Homework ! This should be standard in EVERY school.
The teacher prepares homework, then puts it online on a special platform - pupils later , in the afternoon or whenever they like to do it, go online and do their homework at home, on their computers and completely on their own.

Co-operation and participation are key-words that are most important in our future, probably of gaining importance. Both should be integrated in education and play an immanent role already for 10-years-old.
Technology enhanced learning certainly offers a bride variety of concepts, think of university's "blackboards" and so on.

A constructivist view of learning would help.

REALITY IN MEDIA:
POVERTY AS A MEDIA EXPERIENCE

An American website named "pimpthisbum.com" has shown to me, that when it comes to media, and especially when it comes to web 2.0, a lot of things seem to be possible. This is a matter of fact - and it is not necessarily always positive.
However, in this case it can be considered as positive, even though certain aspects occur to be at least critical relating to the way of showing Tim ("the bum"). "Bum" is in no way a respectful term for a homeless man. But of course one can argue, that it is "part of the concept": a respectless term as an attention-catcher to gather a lot of users and donators.

Media used by teachers for their work with young people must suit the children's or teenagers' age, first of all for a better understanding.

"Pimpthisbum.com" for instance is very likely too far out of young people's experience realm – but also children's media often come to deal with poverty and present this to their young audiences in a way they can understand it. Normally they focus so-called "Third-World-Countries" to make poverty a topic for young people. But in my opinion there's a change to be noticed for media stressing this topic also for Europe.
Writers have always been showing "another experience realm" of childhood – because also children experience poverty. Media certainly can't ignore this.

The poor shall not remain "invisible" - to make poverty a (media) topic is also some kind of social inclusion. It's a first step.

"PRODUSAGE"

Web 2.0 is a tool that can help to make a difference, and we should use it for good.
Axel Bruns comes to the point that "Web 2.0 is the business revolution in the computer industry caused by the move to the internet as platform, and an attempt to understand the rules for success on that new platform" (Bruns 2008, 3).

He speaks of produsage - the term produsage relates to the disappearance of the roles of producer and user as such, the classic description of these roles have long disappeared and a clear distinction has faded.
He also points out that produsage is "a wider context of new and emerging concepts for describing the social, technological, and economic environment of user-led content creation" (Bruns 2008, 2).

Naturally web 2.0 cannot be compared to traditional media, even though there are users that are in their jobs journalists, writers and so on and that want to present special topics or content like texts out of a book to a public (often only "their" audiences) this way.
Lots of media people use web 2.0 for topics they cannot take care of the way they wanted to in their jobs. Having written and published an article not always ends a topic.
But also "private users" feel that web 2.0 is something to be taken serious, that it is a tool of worth.

Citizen Journalism opens new spaces for journalism and society.

In all his forms it has "emerged and developed during the first decade of the twenty-first century... driven by similar motivations: it, too, acts as a corrective and a supplement to the output of commercial, industrial journalism" (Bruns 2008, 69). It should never be underestimated in its role as opinion maker and innovation leader. And: it's the same with open source and its products, blogs and so on.

Web 2.0 has a lot of advantages, for those creating media as well as for those, who want to "use" media in some way or another, who want to participate and interact. The so-called "next generation of news consumers" expects to be part of the game, part of media contents in some way. As Shane Bowman points out, kids today have other expectations than kids decades before. They expect to interact with their media (Bowman 2003), and this is a change in Peoples' expectations they have in media, that will certainly develop. There is no way back to the time, when media was just consumed, as kind of a one-way-street, without real opportunity to cling oneself in into the process of communication, without the chance of getting into interaction.

Conclusion

In this contribution I tried to show off the importance of eInclusion out of two perspectives - the first perspective is taking a look at school: Students from all social backgrounds must have the possibility of developing at least good competencies in ICT and the use of online-learning tools. Apart from that it's important that the development of good media-competencies becomes part of the curriculum in schools. Schools should feel obliged to help students develop media-competencies as well as develop knowledge in maths, ethics or biology!

Media have come to play an immanent role in our society. We cannot ignore that students should learn how to make good use of media (online media as well as so-called traditional media like e.g. TV!) and become able to recognise chances and risks.

The second perspective is dealing with the inclusion of poverty as a topic. The poor shall not remain "invisible" - as well as students from all social backgrounds should have the chance to get a good education, poverty should be a topic that's presented in media in an authentic way.

Bibliography:

Banks, John A.L. (2007). Negotiating Participatory Culture in the New Media Environment: Auran and the Trainz Online Community – An (Im)possible Relation. Melbourne DAC 2003 Proceedings, http://hypertext.rmit.edu.au/dac/papers/Banks.pdf , 8 - 12

Baumgartner, P., Häfele, H., Maier-Häfele, K. (2002). e-Learning Praxishandbuch - Auswahl von Lernplattformen. Innsbruck – Wien: Studienverlage.

Bowman, Shane (2003). We Media: How Audiences Are Shaping the Future of News and Information. (Reston, Va.: The Media Center at the American Press Institute, 2003), http://www.hypergene.net/wemedia/download/we_media.pdf (accessed 26 May 2008)

Bruns, Axel (2008). BLOGS, WIKIPEDIA, SECOND LIFE and BEYOND. From Production to Produsage. New York: Peter Lang Publishing, Inc.

Ebner, Martin (2009). Technology Enhanced Learning. TU Graz: e-book. http://elearningblog.tugraz.at/open-content (accessed December 8th 2009)

Frey-Vor, Gerlinde/ Schumacher, Gerlinde (Eds.) (2006). Kinder und Medien 2003/2004. Eine Studie der ARD/ZDF-Medienkommission. Baden-Baden: Nomos Verlagsgesellschaft.

Jewitt, Carey (2006). Technology, Literacy and Learning. A multimodal approach. London and New York: Routledge.

Kinder, Marsha [Ed.] : Kids' media culture / ed. by Marsha Kinder. - Durham, NC [u.a.] : Duke Univ. Press, 1999

Livingstone, Sonia M. [Ed.] . Kids online : opportunities and risks for children / edited by Sonia Livingstone & Leslie Haddon. - Bristol : Policy, 2009.

Paus-Haase, Ingrid/ Lampert, Claudia/ Süss, Daniel (Eds.) (2002). Medienpädagogik in der Kommunikationswissenschaft. Positionen, Perspektiven, Potenziale. Wiesbaden: Westdeutscher Verlag.

Paus-Hasebrink, Ingrid/ Bichler, Michelle (2008).
Mediensozialisationsforschung. Theoretische Fundierung und Fallbeispiel sozial
benachteiligte Kinder. Innsbruck: Studienverlag.

Paus-Hasebrink, Ingrid (2009). Zur Relevanz von sozialer Ungleichheit im
Kontext der Mediensozialisationsforschung. In: Medienpädagogik. Zeitschrift
für Theorie und Praxis der Medienbildung. ISSN 1424-3636. Themenheft Nr.17
Medien und soziokulturelle Unterschiede. (abgerufen am 15.12.2009)
http://www.medienpaed.com/17/paus-hasebrink0905.pdf

Paus-Hasebrink, Ingrid/ Dürager, Andrea/ Wijnen, Christine/ Ugur, Kadri
(2009). Making use of ICT for learning in European schools. In: Livingstone,
Sonia/ Haddon, Leslie (Hrsg.): Kids online. Opportunities and Risks for
Children. Bristol: The Policy Press, S. 217-228.

Schwetz, Herbert/ Zeyringer, Martina/ Reiter, Anton (Hrsg.) (2009).
Konstruktives Lernen mit neuen Medien. Beiträge zu einer konstruktivistischen
Mediendidaktik. Reflexionen zur internationalen Veranstaltung „Neues Lernen
für die Informationsgesellschaft" (9.-11.10.2000) an der Pädagogischen
Akademie des Bundes in Graz. Innsbruck-Wien-München-Bozen:
Studienverlag.

Young people, ICTS and (online) media - Links:

http://www.ictcomenius.eu/
The topic of this EU-Project is connected with information and communication
technologies (ICT) using at schools process, out-off-school activities. The
project is provided for collaboration of 7 schools from 6 countries and will be
supported jointly by at least 157 international mobilities.

www.kiku.at
"Kinderkurier" (KIKU) is for young audiences of the paper Kurier in Vienna.
Kiku offers kids the opportunity of getting an insight in "how a paper is made",
kids can write stories etc.

http://www.kindermuseum.at/kinder/?goto=science
Kids' Museum Vienna offers topics from mostly natural sciences for a young
audience and the opportunity of blogging (children can create their own blogs)

http://www.pimpthisbum.com

www.wuwawi.com
Salzburgs paper "Salzburger Nachrichten" reserves this space for Salzburgs
children - here they can send articles to and stories, write book-reviews, or
discuss new books…

Career: I started as a teenager to work as a journalist at the students' paper and
the city-magazine "Klipp" in Graz/ Austria, several participations at the Youth-
Literature-Workshops in Graz. As a student at the University of Salzburg I
wrote for the girls-magazine "Minnie" / Ehapa-Verlag in Germany,
Rupertusblatt Salzburg and other media, tutor at the University of Salzburg
(ICT&S Center), scientific associate at the Austrian Institute European Legal
Policy Institute. 2002 first publication of my children's book "Papa, der
Drache". 2011 first publication of the book "Geschichten von Max, Marlena und
ihren Freunden" by Bernadette Maria and Maximilian Kaufmann. Currently I
am working on my next book.